STATE OF AFFAIRS:
NATIVE AMERICANS
IN THE 21ST CENTURY

LIFE ON THE
RESERVATIONS

TAMMY GAGNE

Mitchell Lane
PUBLISHERS

P.O. Box 196
Hockessin, Delaware 19707
Visit us on the web: www.mitchelllane.com
Comments? Email us: mitchelllane@mitchelllane.com

STATE OF AFFAIRS:
NATIVE AMERICANS
IN THE 21st CENTURY

Preserving Their Heritage
Native Americans and the Government
Native American Industry in Contemporary America
Life on the Reservations

Printing   1   2   3   4   5   6   7   8   9

PUBLISHER'S NOTE: The facts on which the story
in this book is based have been thoroughly
researched. Documentation of such research
can be found on page 45. While every possible
effort has been made to ensure accuracy, the
publisher will not assume liability for damages
caused by inaccuracies in the data, and
makes no warranty on the accuracy of the
information contained herein.

ABOUT THE AUTHOR:
Tammy Gagne has written numerous books for
adults and children, including *A Kid's Guide
to the Voting Process* and *The Power of the
States* for Mitchell Lane Publishers. She counts
American history and civics among her many
interests. She resides in northern New England
with her husband and son. One of her favorite
pastimes is visiting schools to speak to kids
about the writing process.

Library of Congress
Cataloging-in-Publication Data
Gagne, Tammy.
 Life on the reservations / by Tammy Gagne.
    pages cm. — (State of affairs: native
Americans in the 21st century)
 Includes bibliographical references and index.
 ISBN 978-1-61228-444-6 (library bound)
 1. Indian reservations—United States—Juvenile
literature. 2. Indians of North America—Social
life and customs—21st century. I. Title.
 E93.G34 2013
 970.004'97—dc23
                                                    2013012557

eBook ISBN: 9781612285054

PLB

CONTENTS

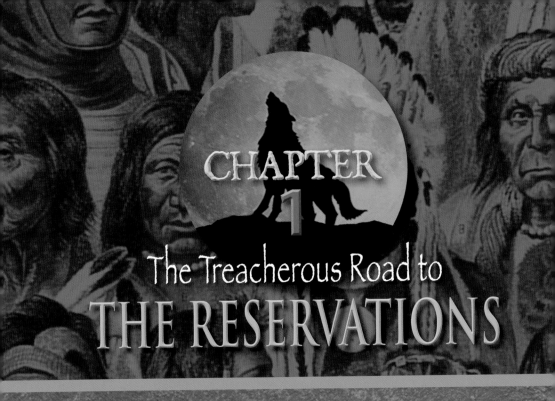

CHAPTER 1

The Treacherous Road to
THE RESERVATIONS

It's Monday morning, and seventeen-year-old Stephanie is getting ready to head to school. Her day will be much like that of other kids her age. She has a big history test on the agenda this afternoon, she is scheduled to work a four-hour shift this evening, and she is already looking forward to the weekend. She will be taking her SATs on Saturday, but Friday night will be a time for celebration. Her tribe's annual powwow is scheduled to start at sunset. Stephanie lives on an Indian reservation. For now, she also goes to school there, but soon she will apply to college.

If she attends a nearby university, she will be able to stay on the reservation and help her family. Stephanie's mother has been out of work for the past year. Her father has a job at a local mine, but money is still tight. Stephanie uses the money from her part-time job to help pay the bills. If she can earn a scholarship to a good college, she could help her parents even more after she graduates. But she worries about how her parents

Semira Crank grew up in Montezuma Creek, a small southeastern Utah community on the Navajo Nation Reservation. She went on to become a student at the College of Engineering at Utah State University. She is believed to be one of the first Native American women to attend the school.

Some of the poorest people in the United States live on the reservations. Many live without electricity, running water, and telephones.

will get by while she's gone. Perhaps she would be a bigger help if she went to a nearby school while living at home. It is a common dilemma for many teens on reservations.

Out of the 313 million people who live in the United States, only about 1.7 percent of them are Native Americans.[1] It doesn't sound like many people at first. When we do the math, though, we realize that this small percentage actually represents more than five million people. The majority of Native Americans live in the same areas of the country as other Americans do. But about 22 percent—more than a million of them—live on reservations.[2]

At the beginning of the nineteenth century, white Americans were moving further into the South. As they settled in this region, they came into contact with large groups of Native Americans including the Cherokee, Creek, Choctaw, Chicasaw, and Seminole tribes. These Native Americans lived on land that the white settlers wanted for growing crops like cotton. The

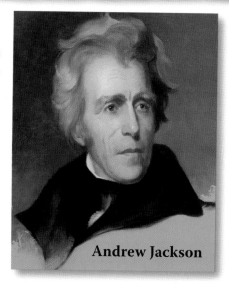

Andrew Jackson

solution the white Americans came up with was to remove the native people from the area.

A man named Andrew Jackson was the Tennessee state militia's major general. He supported the idea of removing the Indians, as they were called, with great passion. In 1814, Jackson led the Battle of Horseshoe Bend against the Creek people. The tribe lost more than 22 million acres of land in southern Georgia and central Alabama as a result of its defeat in this fight.[3] Over the next several years, Jackson and his men also forced tribes in Mississippi and western Tennessee to surrender land to the United States as well.

Like the Creek tribe, the Seminole people did their best to defend their land. They did not fight alone, however. Surviving Creek tribe members and escaped African American slaves who had been living among the Seminole also took part in the First Seminole War. The slaves' involvement angered the white settlers even further. Even with this extra help, the Seminole were no match for Jackson's army.

Over the next decade, Jackson formed treaties with other Native American tribes. These agreements gave the United States more land in the east and provided the tribes with land in the west. By 1824, the United States had taken control of three-quarters of Alabama and Florida. They had also acquired Native American land in Georgia, Tennessee, Mississippi, Kentucky, and North Carolina.

In 1828, Jackson was elected president of the United States. Although his title had changed again, his desire for Native American land had not. And now he had even more reason to want it. Not only was the land in the South ideal for growing cotton, but large amounts of gold had also been found in Georgia.

Jackson passed the Indian Removal Act in 1830. This new law stated that Indians who wanted to remain in the east would become citizens of their states. The ones who did not want to become citizens would receive land to the west of the Mississippi River in exchange for leaving. Those who agreed to the conditions would be treated peacefully. Those who did not would be forced to leave.

Many tribes knew that they could not defend their homes if the warfare continued. If they left, they would have land of their own. They did not want to fight with white Americans any longer. Over time, an overwhelming number of Native Americans left the southeast and moved to new territories in the area that is now Oklahoma.

The Cherokee people gradually adapted to the ways of the white settlers. By the 1830s, many of them had learned how to speak and write English. They also began farming the land the way the Europeans did. They lived in houses that looked just like the homes of the whites. They even adopted Christianity as their religion. Eventually, though, it became clear that no matter

Many Native Americans who traveled the Trail of Tears did not survive the forced migration.

what these Natives Americans did, it would never be enough. By 1838, the Cherokee were also removed from the east.

The Cherokee refer to their forced migration westward as the Trail of Tears. This trip was a difficult one filled with pain and struggle. The people were hungry and tired, and many of them got sick along the way. Of the fifteen thousand Cherokee that made the journey, more than four thousand died.[4]

Disputes over Native American land and the right to govern it continued through the twentieth century. Some disputes even continue to this day. Native Americans are both citizens of the United States and members of their own tribal nations. This creates many gray areas when it comes to laws. A great number of cases involving tribal lands have made their way to the US Supreme Court over the last two hundred years.

Former principal chief of the Cherokee Nation, Chad Smith has said that even today some politicians want to see the Cherokee Nation's rights terminated. "History does have a way of repeating itself," he says, "and we are once again at a point in history where impending doom lurks on the horizon. One hundred years from now, we want to have what we had one hundred years ago. One hundred years ago our nation had an enriching cultural identity, our government and our citizens had economic self-reliance and a strong, sovereign government that protected our people."[5]

Like Smith, many Cherokee think the most important issues for the reservations today are language, jobs, and community. The Cherokee language will soon be at risk of disappearing if more classes for young people aren't put in place. The Cherokee people also need jobs, and many also need the proper skills and training to get hired. Bringing people together to accomplish these important goals is vital.

By the time Smith left office in 2011, he had made some large advances, and he is quick to share the credit. He recalls, "I recruited some very, very good people and told them, 'This is what we need to accomplish. Go and do it. Come to me if you

Chad Smith

need help with gathering resources.' Everything we've touched has increased."[6]

Cherokee Nation Businesses now owns and operates eight casinos, as well as numerous other companies that have created jobs for the Cherokee people. Smith also helped strengthen the Cherokee Nation's healthcare system. It is now the largest of its kind in the country.

Smith's proudest moment came when he attended a girls' basketball game at Sequoyah High School. While there, he overheard two girls behind him speaking to each other in Cherokee. He insists, "I couldn't have asked for anything more."[7]

Even with recent advancements, life on the reservations today isn't easy. More than a quarter of the Native Americans who call these tribal lands their home live in poverty. Limited education, employment, health care, and housing are ongoing problems in Cherokee Nation, Navajo Nation (the largest reservation in the United States), and the other reservations across the country. Many reservation families live without electricity, running water, and telephones—conveniences that most other Americans take for granted.

At the same time, there is a lot of pride on the reservations. Native Americans have not forgotten their past. Their challenge now is to hold onto their history and culture while moving with the rest of the country into the twenty-first century.

TRIBE MEMBERS WHO REMAINED IN THE EAST

Life for the Native Americans who chose to stay in the east after the Indian Removal Act proved to be much more difficult than they had expected. For decades, the Choctaw people in Mississippi tried to adapt to non-Native American society, but it just didn't work. In 1939, more than fifteen thousand acres of land were purchased to create a reservation for this tribe, but it would be several more years before it became official.

Today tribal councils govern the reservations, but the early versions of these governing bodies had very little authority. They couldn't create laws, and they couldn't make decisions about money. Before they could gain these powers, the Choctaw people had to create a constitution, the foundation for their new government. The United States accepted the document in 1945, officially recognizing the Mississippi Band of Choctaw Indians. The constitution was then ratified through a vote of the Choctaw tribal members.

The first thing the band did was elect an official tribal council. It consisted of sixteen members. They then chose one member to act as their chairman. Joe Chitto of the Standing Pine Community was the first person to serve in this position. Council members were elected for two-year terms.

During the 1970s, the Choctaw tribe amended its constitution to make two changes. First, the group decided that tribal chiefs would be elected by the people. This meant that the government now had both an executive and a legislative branch. Second, the tribe extended the length of each council member's term from two years to four.

Choctaw Nation seal

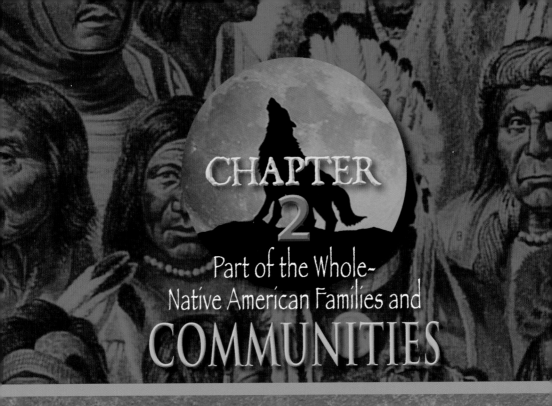

CHAPTER 2

Part of the Whole~
Native American Families and
COMMUNITIES

Family plays a large role in life on the reservations. Native American families on these tribal lands are a lot like families in other parts of the United States. Some are nuclear families, consisting of a mother, a father, and children. Others are made up of a single parent and kids. It is quite common on the reservations for both types of families to also include extended family members. Grandparents, aunts, uncles, and cousins often live under the same roof with nuclear family members. This is true of Native American families both on and off the reservations, but it is seen even more frequently on tribal lands.

Native Americans have a strong sense of responsibility when it comes to family. Younger generations usually see caring for their aging parents and grandparents as their duty. The reasons go much deeper than mere obligation, however. Most members of the younger generations want their relatives to be proud of them. Like other American families, Native American families also want their children to do well in life.

This family lives on the Hopi Reservation in Arizona. It is very common for Native American families like this one to live together in the same household. In many cases several generations may live under the same roof.

A study published in the *Journal for Higher Education* discusses the drive of Native American students to earn their college degrees. Family was among the most common reasons the students listed as their motivation to pursue higher education. One student shared, "I'm the first in my family to go to college, and so it will mean a lot to my family and me if I can graduate and become a teacher."[1]

Another student who listed family as their biggest motivation shared, "We have a close-knit family, extended family. . . . My greatest fear is to let them down right now."[2] Many students said that their family support is so strong that it has even helped them overcome difficult situations. College can be a tough time for any young person, but it can be especially hard for Native Americans. Due to limited resources on the reservations, young people are often less prepared for the academic demands of

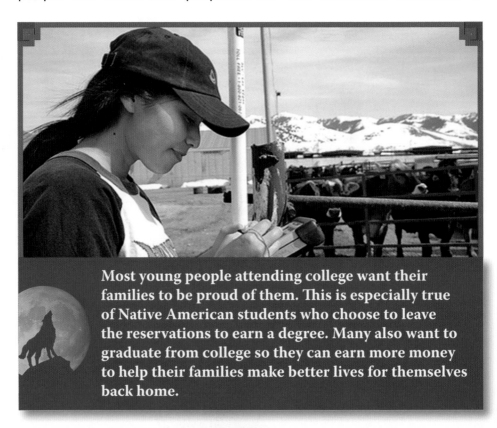

Most young people attending college want their families to be proud of them. This is especially true of Native American students who choose to leave the reservations to earn a degree. Many also want to graduate from college so they can earn more money to help their families make better lives for themselves back home.

college than other students are. Many Native American families also struggle to pay for their children's education. The students from this study said that the chance to make life better for their families is what motivates them to overcome these obstacles and earn their degrees.

Native American families teach their children that the group is more important than the individual. Many of the students said that they wanted to go back to their reservations after graduation to help their own people. One student admitted, "I have a lot of family that still live on the reservation, and most of my cousins don't have high school degrees. . . . Maybe I can serve as a role model or make them proud of what I have been doing and of my achievements, serve as a driving force."[3]

Giving something back to the community is an important part of life on the reservations. In most cities and towns across the United States, communities join together during a difficult time, such as a serious illness or death. Following a funeral, family and friends often send flowers or take casseroles to the family of the deceased. On some reservations, it is the grieving family who gives gifts to the other community members. They do this as a way to thank their friends and neighbors for being there for them throughout the difficult time.

As close as Native American communities may be, they are not without their problems. High dropout rates, alcoholism, and drug abuse are among the biggest issues affecting Native Americans living on the reservations. Native American men are 50 percent more likely to suffer from problems with alcohol than other men in the United States. Alcohol and drug use is one of the top three causes of death among young Native Americans.[4]

Alcohol threatens the health of many Native Americans even before they are born. Native American mothers who drink while they are pregnant put their children at risk for fetal alcohol syndrome. This condition can lead to problems with a child's attention span, learning, and memory. It can even cause issues with hearing and vision. These problems can last a lifetime, and they aren't the only negative effects of a parent who abuses alcohol.

According to Colorado State University's Tri-Ethnic Center, the behavior of Native American parents has a powerful effect on their children when it comes to their use of alcohol and other drugs. Native American teens with parents who abuse alcohol are more likely to drink themselves as early as age thirteen. They are also more likely to suffer from alcohol-related problems by the age of eighteen.[5]

Native Americans who practice traditional spiritual beliefs are less likely to have problems with drugs and alcohol.

Certainly, families and communities have a great deal of influence on their younger members. In many cases, though, this influence can be a positive one. A study conducted by Arizona State University revealed that young Native Americans who practice the traditional spiritual beliefs of their culture are less likely to use both alcohol and drugs.[6]

To many Native Americans, the idea of community is both large and small. Each year, thousands of people come together

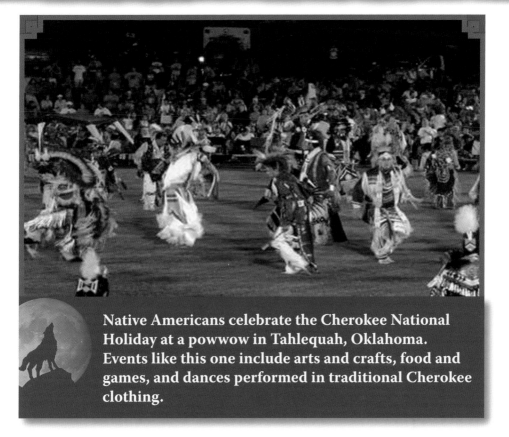

Native Americans celebrate the Cherokee National Holiday at a powwow in Tahlequah, Oklahoma. Events like this one include arts and crafts, food and games, and dances performed in traditional Cherokee clothing.

to celebrate the Cherokee National Holiday. This event is held on the anniversary of the adoption of their tribe's constitution. The holiday includes arts and crafts, food, games, a parade, a powwow, and other traditional activities.

Star Oosahwe attended one such event with her family members, Sarah Oosahwee and Sedelta Oosahwee. Although their names are spelled slightly differently, all three young women are related. They competed together in a blowgun contest, a sport that has traditionally been a man's sport in Cherokee culture.

"There's a lot of men in one generation, then a lot of women in the next, so the men really encouraged us," Star explains. "Our family does this at family functions."[7] She enjoyed taking part in a sport that her ancestors played.

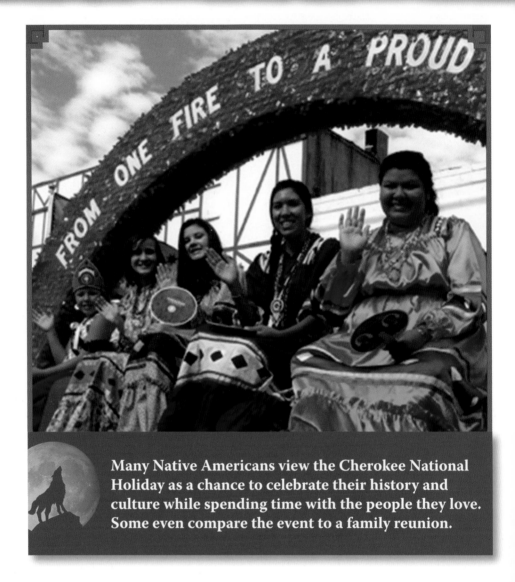

Many Native Americans view the Cherokee National Holiday as a chance to celebrate their history and culture while spending time with the people they love. Some even compare the event to a family reunion.

Sarah adds, "I enjoy it because I get to be part of the culture, and it's fun to do it with my family and spend time with them."[8] All three young women said that they see the Cherokee National Holiday as a big family reunion.

A MODERN FAMILY TRADITION

Basketball is a popular family pastime in Navajo Nation. Whether play is limited to shooting hoops in the backyard or it involves an organized team, it always seems to draw a crowd. High school basketball teams on these tribal lands are often very successful. These teams frequently make it into playoff games in big cities like Albuquerque, New Mexico, or Phoenix, Arizona. Fans travel hundreds of miles to see their favorite teams participate in these events.

Very few Native American athletes have made it all the way to professional courts, but the ones that have are celebrated by the people. Ryneldi Becenti is one of them. Before she entered the WNBA in 1997, Becenti played for Arizona State University. While she was on the school's team, her fellow teammates would often comment about the large number of fans that attended games to see her play. In previous seasons, the young women had often played to half-empty gymnasiums. With Becenti there, however, there was hardly ever an available seat.

Growing up, Ryneldi Becenti wanted to play basketball day and night. She often did so with only the moon and stars for light.

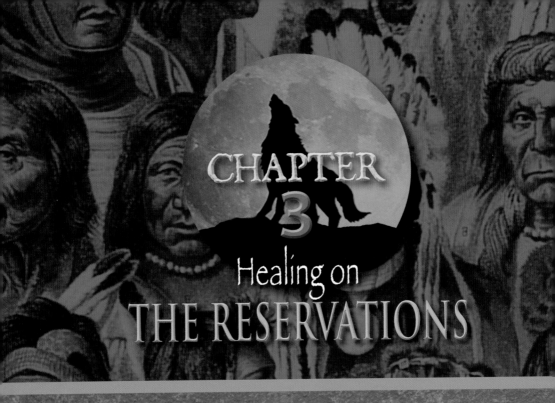

CHAPTER 3

Healing on
THE RESERVATIONS

Life on the reservations today is a unique blending of the old ways and modern technology. Interestingly, the twenty-first century has brought many tribe members back to their traditional Native American culture. They look to the customs of their ancestors to help guide them through the challenges of their everyday lives.

Nowhere is this combination of old and new more obvious than in a hospital. Tuba City Regional Health Care Corporation is located on the Navajo reservation in Tuba City, Arizona. This modern medical center provides its patients with state-of-the-art health care. It also offers them the opportunity to be seen by medicine men. These traditional Native American healers perform ceremonies to rid patients of bad spirits. They also use songs and prayers to bless the rooms in which previous patients have died.

Even modern doctors respect the old ways. Dr. Joachim Chino is a Navajo-Acoma who grew up on the reservation. He is now

Tuba City Regional Health Care Corporation offers patients a unique mix of treatment options. A person may receive state-of-the-art medical treatment from a medical doctor in a room that has been blessed by a traditional Native American medicine man. Both approaches to healing are respectful of each other in this setting.

the chief of surgery at the hospital and thinks that respecting cultural beliefs is an important part of his job. This can put him in a difficult position at times. For example, many Navajo people believe that actually saying that a person has an illness is like wishing him or her harm. When Dr. Chino must deliver bad news, he speaks in the third person, using the word "patient" instead of saying "you." In situations like this, he also only talks about chances for survival if the patients specifically ask him about them.

"It just delays their fear—not mentioning death and dying specifically in their situation," Dr. Chino explains. "I think it's helpful."[1] He points out, though, that the medical care he gives his patients is no different than the care they would receive from other surgeons.

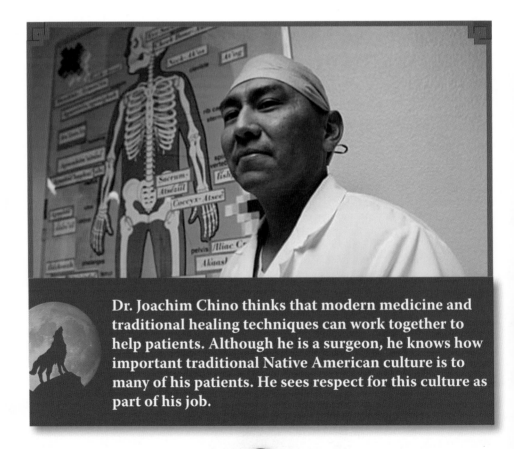

Dr. Joachim Chino thinks that modern medicine and traditional healing techniques can work together to help patients. Although he is a surgeon, he knows how important traditional Native American culture is to many of his patients. He sees respect for this culture as part of his job.

Medicine men likewise respect the modern ways. Sometimes a patient who is seen by a traditional healer needs modern treatment, such as surgery. Many Native Americans feel more comfortable having surgery with the blessing of a traditional healer.

Dr. Chino also makes a point of avoiding direct eye contact with his patients. To many non-Native Americans, it may seem rude to not look someone in the eye when speaking to him or her. In traditional Native American culture, however, staring directly into a person's eyes is considered disrespectful, especially when dealing with someone older than oneself.

The respect between modern caregivers and medicine men goes both ways. David Begay is one of these medicine men. He thinks that patients turn to him to rediscover their spiritual roots. He also thinks that it's important for them to receive modern treatments. "Any way to get healed, any way to get help, I think that's the ultimate thinking here," he shares.[2]

When Dr. Chino was growing up, medicine men would see patients before modern doctors treated them. Today the order is

Traditional Native American healers can also be found outside of hospitals. This medicine man is creating a sandpainting as part of a healing ceremony for a young girl who has come to seek his help.

usually reversed. Patients rarely see both types of caregivers at the same time. The one exception is when a new baby is born. When a woman comes to the hospital to give birth, the traditional and modern healers come together. A medicine man will perform a ceremony while a midwife helps the mother-to-be deliver the baby. The medicine man focuses on easing any complications and creating an environment of beauty, harmony, and strength for the new arrival. If any problems do arise, the medical staff is prepared to deal with them with modern medicine.

The old and new ways don't always work together without conflict. Sometimes the advice of the medicine man will interfere with the doctor's orders. For instance, a patient may need to return for a follow-up visit with a doctor and be told by a medicine man not to cross over water. If the person has strong traditional beliefs, he or she may be hesitant to come to the appointment if it means crossing a bridge along the way.

Traditional Native American medicine isn't only about religion. Separating the spiritual aspects of the old ways from the more practical side of these methods can be difficult, though. Traditional Native American healing is a form of *holistic* medicine. The word holistic means "whole." This type of healing, which has become increasingly popular in the United States in recent years, involves treating the whole person. Both holistic caregivers and traditional Native American healers believe that a person's mind, body, and spirit are connected and must be treated together.

Traditional Native American treatment may consist of using herbs or other plants to cure an illness. Treating the mind and spirit is also an important part of the process. Medicine men typically spend more time with their patients than modern doctors do, asking questions to get to the spiritual or emotional root of a problem. Most people on the reservations rely on traditional medicine for treating minor illnesses. If these methods don't work, however, they often turn to modern ways.

More studies need to be performed on Native American healing before we will know how effective it is. The American

Medicine men spend a great deal of time with their patients, learning about both the person and the problem. They may instruct patients to use plants or herbs to cure the physical parts of a problem. Treating the mind and spirit is also an important aspect of traditional healing.

Cancer Society's website states, "Although Native American healing has not been proven to cure disease, individual reports suggest that it can reduce pain and stress and improve quality of life. The communal and spiritual support provided by this type of healing could have helpful effects. Prayers, introspection, and meditation can be calming and can help to reduce stress."[3]

HEALING OLD WOUNDS

Native Americans from various reservations across the United States often suffer from common problems. These issues aren't physical. Instead they relate to mental well-being. Some doctors think the common link is the troubled history these people share. Dr. Ann Bullock practices family medicine in Cherokee, North Carolina. She explains, "There's been an unusual amount of trauma that has happened to Indian people and there are very clear physiologic as well as behavioral responses to trauma."[4]

As horrific as it was, it may seem odd that an experience like the Trail of Tears could still be affecting Native Americans more than a century after it happened, but that is exactly what some experts think is happening. Dr. Carrie Johnson is a psychologist on the opposite side of the country in Los Angeles, California, but she sees the same pattern in her patients. "A lot of our children that we see, for example, have been through not only one trauma but often multiple traumas in their life. . . . But then when we look at multi-generational trauma, we look at what has happened to their parents, or what has happened to their grandparents, or their great-grandparents, and how that has been passed on from generation to generation."[5]

People who endure traumatic situations often suffer from a condition called post-traumatic stress disorder (PTSD). This illness is linked with high rates of alcohol and drug abuse, anxiety disorders, depression, and even violence in those who suffer from it. "When people have been traumatized, they pass it on," reports Dr. Bullock. Parents suffering from PTSD often pass their problems on to their children. "It's not because parents don't want to try or because they're not trying because they don't care. It's because they can't."[6]

There is help available, however. Counseling and even traditional tribal ceremonies are being used to break the dangerous cycle of PTSD among Native Americans. Both modern doctors and traditional healers agree that the best approach is to bring the matter out in the open so this part of Native American history can stop repeating itself.

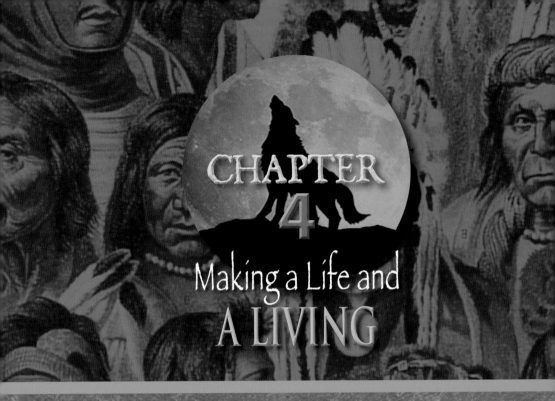

CHAPTER 4

Making a Life and
A LIVING

Like other parts of the United States, the reservations suffered a significant loss of jobs in the years following the financial crisis of 2007-2008. Finding steady work became harder and harder for many Native Americans living on tribal lands. On the Navajo reservation, which includes land in three western states, the unemployment rate was nearly 50 percent in 2013.[1] In order to survive, many people were forced to move to areas with more opportunities. Their departure actually made it more difficult for the remaining tribe members to climb out of poverty. With fewer people to support their economies, these Native Americans have an even harder time improving the conditions on the reservations.

For those who are fortunate enough to find work on the reservations, their jobs often pay much less than the same job would have paid just a few years ago. For people who have no job, though, working for less is better than not working at all. Robert Black is a chapter manager, similar to a city manager, on the Navajo reservation. He points out, "It's not too surprising if

Monument Valley in the Navajo Nation is a very beautiful place. To outsiders it may seem like a wonderful place to live and work. Unfortunately, it is also one of the hardest places for Native Americans to find work.

you see a guy who's normally making $25 an hour, who says, 'I'll settle for $9 for a couple weeks so I can have some gas money to carry me over to my next job.' "[2]

Many Native Americans manage to make their livings as artisans, but they rely heavily on tourist dollars. With much of the country struggling to make ends meet, there is far less money to be spent on vacations or even day trips to the reservations. Without these customers, a large amount of Native American arts and crafts sit in shops unsold.

For most rural towns on the reservations, times are harder than ever, but many urban areas are doing remarkably well. Even through the poor economy, reservations with large casinos and hotels are thriving. The answer for the rural reservations might seem obvious: Create tourist attractions there as well. Unfortunately, doing this isn't as easy as it sounds. Big businesses like these require a large amount of start-up cash.

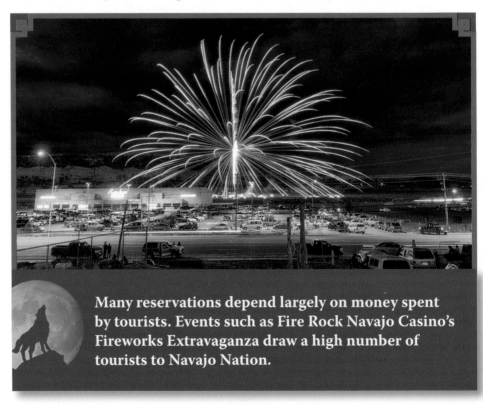

Many reservations depend largely on money spent by tourists. Events such as Fire Rock Navajo Casino's Fireworks Extravaganza draw a high number of tourists to Navajo Nation.

Startup cash is hard to come by on the reservations. Grants are available, but getting one can be a very difficult process. Because of this, many Native American vendors simply set up shop on the side of the road.

Federal grants are available for economic development, but applying for them can be difficult and time consuming. Many Navajo people had hoped that the billions of dollars in stimulus money from the government would help them build centers for art and entertainment. Actually getting the money, however, also proved to be a long and complicated process. Before the funds were made available, increasing poverty made it necessary for this federal money to be spent on other, more basic things.

Harvard professor Joseph Kalt explains, "The federal government itself has estimated that the backlog of unmet needs—just basic infrastructure, old school buildings, water and sewer—is much, much larger than the kinds of funds that have been made available to Indian country."[3]

Grants and stimulus money can help, but this type of money can only do so much, especially when it is in short supply. The reservations need investors—people willing to supply money to create new businesses. Finding these investors can be difficult. Many Native Americans think one of their best resources is their youth. Young people who graduate with business degrees can help by putting them to use on the reservations. This solution isn't quite as simple as it seems, however.

Young Native Americans who grow up on reservations may plan to come back to their hometowns after college. Many of them truly want to give something back to the people who raised them and the people who share their culture. Getting that education and making enough money are often the biggest challenges. Many families can't afford to send their children to universities. Of the students who are lucky enough to receive loans or scholarships, many of them find it difficult to make a living on the reservations after graduation. In order to give something back, they must first find jobs that pay well and then save money.

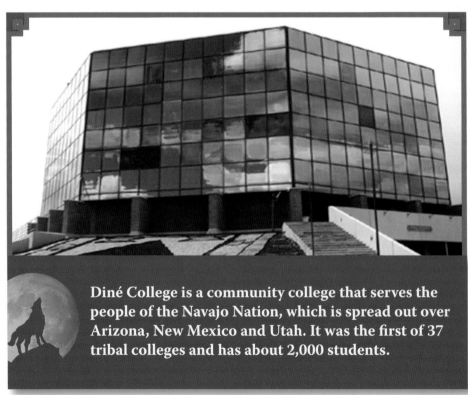

Diné College is a community college that serves the people of the Navajo Nation, which is spread out over Arizona, New Mexico and Utah. It was the first of 37 tribal colleges and has about 2,000 students.

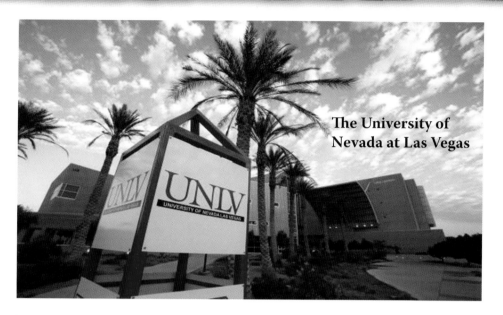

The University of
Nevada at Las Vegas

The University of Nevada at Las Vegas (UNLV) is helping Native Americans get an education by letting them learn from home. UNLV offers a distance-learning master's degree program for people interested in careers in the hotel, hospitality, and food and beverage industries. Stephanie Meeder is a front office manager for the Cherokee Casino Resort and Hotel. She graduated from this program while working full time.

"I wanted to get a master's degree in hotel management for years, but there was no school in the area that offered a hospitality and hotel management degree," she recalled. "So, I knew I couldn't pass up the opportunity to take graduate classes here."[4]

Doyle Paden is the manager of education and development for Cherokee Casinos. He sees the UNLV program as helping the Native American community in two ways. "The Master's Graduate Program provides education to people that are employees of Cherokee Nation business entities, but it also provides a way to look for future leaders and prepare them for leadership positions."[5]

Brett Isaac is another Native American who is putting his education to use for his people. A graduate of Arizona State University, Isaac is the program director of the Shonto Community

Brett Isaac

Development Corporation on the Navajo reservation. He works to bring big business to the reservation, but admits, "It's not easy on the Navajo Nation when there's so many people, so much land base to cover. Projects like this are very hard to get funded and noticed."[6]

Isaac thinks that it is important for the Navajo people to embrace green living, including solar energy. Coal mines and coal-fired power plants currently provide about 1,500 jobs on the reservation. The air pollution that these plants cause is bound to become a big problem for the plants in the near future. The Environmental Protection Agency (EPA) could insist that they perform updates costing as much as $3 billion. A requirement like this would shut down these businesses and put employees out of work until these extensive changes could be made.

Isaac understands that solving this problem must be done a little at a time. "If they were to close tomorrow, we would be in a whole mess of trouble," he says. "We're to some degree supportive of them continuing operation. The regulations are going to catch up with them and we need to start planning ahead and thinking about the long term."[7]

ADDING THEIR 50 CENT

One of the most popular types of music among young Native Americans is hip-hop. Donald Kelly is the executive director of the Native American Music Awards. When asked about hip-hop music, he reveals, "Among the kids, it's the most popular music on the reservations right now."[8]

Native Americans aren't just listening to hip-hop. They're also performing it. Litefoot is a popular Cherokee rapper who grew up in Oklahoma. Natay is a Navajo rapper from Albuquerque, and Shadowyze is a Creek and Cherokee rapper from Florida. Like other hip-hop artists, these musicians use their lives for inspiration. They sing about the stereotypes they encounter as Native Americans.

Native American record producer Tom Bee explains one reason why rap music is a good fit with this culture. "Native people have a long history of oral tradition. Rap is a new oral tradition for a lot of Native artists."[9]

Still, no Native American rapper has successfully crossed into mainstream music yet. Litefoot did open for Ludacris once, but he received boos when he took the stage. Litefoot knows that making it big won't be easy. "I've got to bring people from a complete state of ignorance about my people to a point of understanding," he admits. "I don't think anybody in hip-hop has a job as tough as mine."[10]

Bee too knows the job will be a difficult one, but he also thinks it will be worthwhile. "There's a lot of talent out there," he says. "There's a next Eminem or Snoop Dogg in Native America. We just need a break."[11]

Litefoot

CHAPTER 5

Merging With
THE WORLD

When the reservations were created over two hundred years ago, many people thought that Native Americans and white citizens should live separate lives. These people assumed that Native Americans were too different from the rest of the country to live together peacefully. The twenty-first century has brought many changes to the reservations, including increasing interest from other Americans of various races. College students from all over the United States can now take classes in Native American studies to learn about the cultures and histories of the various tribes. Some graduates even choose professions that involve making life on the reservations better for the people who live there. Several of them even live or work on the reservations themselves as part of the process.

In 2012, an eleventh grader from Riverview High School in Sarasota, Florida, spent part of his summer vacation with the Eastern Band of Cherokee Indians. John David Kurman traveled to their reservation in the Smoky Mountains of North Carolina to

Many things on the reservations have changed over the last two hundred years, but the beautiful scenery isn't one of them. Places like Mingo Falls on the Cherokee Reservation are as beautiful as ever. Natural attractions like this one bring many tourists to the reservation each year.

volunteer his time at the Kituwah Immersion Academy. The school teaches traditional subjects in Cherokee for students from preschool through second grade. In exchange for his work as a teaching assistant, the school allowed Kurman to study the language of the Cherokee people.

"I spent most of my summers as a kid with my uncle in North Carolina and felt a kind of connection with that area," says Kurman. "I thought it would be interesting to learn the language of the people native to that area and learn more about the culture. . . . It was definitely a big trip for a sixteen-year-old to embark on alone, but I've always had a lot of interest in language and Native American culture, so I was pretty driven to do it."[1]

Kurman is no stranger to learning different languages. In addition to studying Spanish for many years, he is also now learning Arabic and Chinese. Still, he found Cherokee to be a great challenge. "It's by far the most difficult language I could imagine because there are so many different ways of saying things and so many different dialects. I quickly learned that written Cherokee and spoken Cherokee are two very different things. For instance, when it's written out, 'What' is a five syllable word, but no one actually says the whole thing when they're speaking; it's shortened to two, or sometimes even just one, syllable. Sometimes you have to learn three different ways to say one word and that's really tough."[2]

When Kurman wasn't working with the kids, he spent time visiting the local museums and historical landmarks. He even walked part of the Trail of Tears. "I got to go out on my own and do things I never imagined I would while learning about a language most people never get to study."[3] With one more year of high school left, Kurman still wasn't sure what he would do after graduation, but he knew that he wanted a career that would help him put his love of languages to use. Perhaps one day he will return to Kituwah Immersion Academy as a teacher.

Much like Kurman, Native American teens who live on reservations also want to learn about the world outside their home. Many of them travel to other parts of the country during college. Some even travel off the reservations during their high school years. The experience is different for each person, but some young Native American people have found that the rest of the world often stereotypes them.

During the Nineteenth Annual Navajo Studies Conference in New Mexico, the Institute of American Indian Arts held a talk. It was called "Bridging Two Worlds: Preparing for College Beyond the Reservation While Honoring Navajo Culture and Practice." The panel was made up of five Navajo students from St. Michael's Indian School, a Catholic school near Window Rock, Arizona.

One of the teens, Brooke Overturf, spoke about an experience she had when she and several other Navajo students traveled to a Catholic school in Philadelphia, Pennsylvania. She recalled that the kids asked her if she lived in a teepee and whether she hunted buffalo. They wondered aloud if she had ever heard of a cell phone. "They didn't know we have a McDonald's on our reservation," she added.[4]

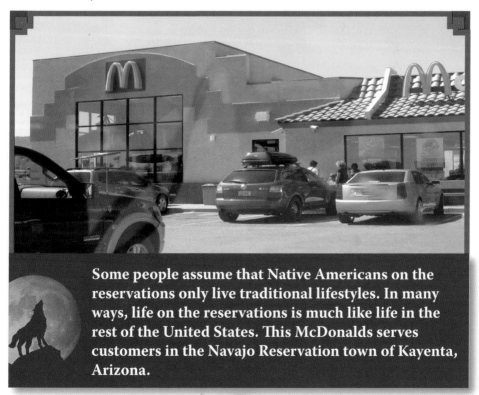

Some people assume that Native Americans on the reservations only live traditional lifestyles. In many ways, life on the reservations is much like life in the rest of the United States. This McDonalds serves customers in the Navajo Reservation town of Kayenta, Arizona.

St. Michael's
Indian School

MacArthur Jones, another Navajo student from the panel, had a similar experience when he traveled to the east coast for a summer training program. Students had come to the event from various parts of the United States, Brazil, China, Germany, and Russia. He confided, "One even asked, 'Where's your feather?' "[5]

The teens also spoke about their drive to learn as much as possible, so they can put their knowledge to work at home. Jones has received a full scholarship to the University of New Mexico, where he plans to study medicine. He told the audience, "My goal is to combine traditional and Western medicine together for the benefit of our people."[6]

A third panelist, Kaitlyn Haskie, also plans to return to the reservation. As she explained, "We're taught to come back, and when I come back, I want to be educated. I strive for knowledge. I want to know more. I want to know all of it. I don't want people to see us as savage. I want people to know we are powerful. We have all this knowledge, and we want to use it for good."[7]

LEAVING THE RESERVATION

Crystal Lee, who studied community health sciences at the University of Nevada, often feels pulled between the Navajo reservation where she grew up and the world outside it. "I feel like I'm learning here in the Western world in terms of my education, but I'm missing out on a lot culturally not being in the Navajo world anymore," she shares. "Both are good, but I still feel a sense of guilt. Still to this day, I struggle with different world views. At the core of me I am a Navajo woman. But that's very different than the Western world in every capacity from my personal to educational to professional life."[8]

In 2010, Lee created United Natives, a mentoring program for young people who are attending college off the reservation. "I didn't know how much work it was going to be, but it's exciting to see it evolve and grow," she states. "The mentors give them support. A lot of students sometimes just need someone to talk to who understands."[9]

Former United States President Bill Clinton recognized United Natives through the Clinton Global Initiative. Like her people, though, Lee is very humble. "I'm just really passionate about helping my tribal people," she said. "My goal in life is to make my community more healthy and assist in any way I can."[10]

The Clinton Global Initiative helped Lee become a voice for young Native Americans on an international level. In 2010, she was appointed co-chairwoman of the United Nations Indigenous Youth Caucus.

Chapter 1

1. United States Census Bureau, *Profile America Facts for Features,* "American Indian and Alaska Native Heritage Month: November 2011," November 1, 2011, http://www.census.gov/newsroom/releases/archives/facts_for_features_special_editions/cb11-ff22.html
2. Native American Aid, "Living Conditions," http://www.nrcprograms.org/site/PageServer?pagename=naa_livingconditions.
3. PBS, *Africans in America,* "Indian Removal," http://www.pbs.org/wgbh/aia/part4/4p2959.html
4. PBS, *Africans in America,* "The Trail of Tears," http://www.pbs.org/wgbh/aia/part4/4h1567.html
5. Amber Wilson, *Tulsa World,* "Cherokee Culture Promoted at National Tribal Holiday," September 5, 2004.
6. Jarrel Wade, *Tulsa World,* "Former Cherokee Principal Chief Chad Smith Looks Back With Pride," October 25, 2011.
7. Ibid.

Chapter 2

1. Raphael M. Guillory and Mimi Wolverton, *The Journal for Higher Education,* "It's About Family: Native American Student Persistence in Higher Education," vol. 79, January/February 2008, p. 74.
2. Ibid.
3. Ibid, p. 75.
4. Emily Narvaes Wilmsen, Colorado State University, "Parental Behavior Regarding Alcohol is a Heavy Influence on American Indian Teenagers, Study Says," June 28, 2011, http://www.news.colostate.edu/Release/5780
5. Ibid.
6. Targeted News Service, "American Indian Spiritual Beliefs Influential in Spurring Youth to Avoid Drugs and Alcohol," August 20, 2012.
7. Amber Wilson, *Tulsa World,* "Cherokee Culture Promoted at National Tribal Holiday," September 5, 2004.
8. Ibid.

Chapter 3

1. Felicia Fonseca and Heather Clark, *USA Today,* "Native American Doctors Blend Modern Care, Medicine Men," September 16, 2010.
2. Ibid.
3. American Cancer Society, "Native American Healing," November 1, 2008, http://www.cancer.org/Treatment/TreatmentsandSideEffects/ComplementaryandAlternativeMedicine/MindBodyandSpirit/native-american-healing

4. PBS, *Indian Country Diaries,* "Historic Trauma May Be Causing Today's Health Crisis," September 2006, http://www.pbs.org/indiancountry/challenges/trauma.html
5. Ibid.
6. Ibid.

Chapter 4
1. Navajo Nation Department of Agriculture, http://www.agriculture.navajo-nsn.gov/
2. Daniel Kraker, National Public Radio, "On Rural Navajo Reservation, Jobs Are Still Scarce," October 21, 2009, http://www.npr.org/templates/story/story.php?storyId=113967186
3. Ibid.
4. David Page, *Journal Record,* "Cherokee Nation Has 13 Oklahoma Students in Masters Degree Program," January 16, 2006.
5. Ibid.
6. Daniel Kraker, National Public Radio, "On Rural Navajo Reservation, Jobs Are Still Scarce," October 21, 2009, http://www.npr.org/templates/story/story.php?storyId=113967186
7. Laurel Morales, Fronteras, "Coal Remains King on Navajo Nation—For Now," October 10, 2011, http://www.fronterasdesk.org/news/2011/oct/10/clean-green-energy-pollution-electricity-plant/
8. Leanne Potts, *Chicago Tribune,* "Hip-Hop Finds Audience on Reservations," December 5, 2004
9. Ibid.
10. Ibid.
11. Ibid.

Chapter 5
1. Jessi Smith, *Herald-Tribune,* "Youth Explores Cherokee Life," September 11, 2012.
2. Ibid.
3. Ibid.
4. Robert Nott, *The Santa Fe New Mexican,* "Navajo Students Discuss Transition to College Outside the Reservation," March 16, 2012.
5. Ibid.
6. Ibid.
7. Ibid.
8. Jessica Fryman, *Las Vegas Review-Journal,* "Cultural Gap Inspires Mentor Group," June 15, 2011.
9. Ibid.
10. Ibid.

Alexie, Sherman. *The Absolutely True Diary of a Part-Time Indian.* New York: Little Brown, 2009.

Kristofic, Jim. *Navajos Wear Nikes: A Reservation Life.* Albuquerque, NM: University of New Mexico Press, 2011.

McIntosh, Marsha. *Growing Up Native.* Broomall, PA: Mason Crest, 2008.

Treuer, Anton. *Everything You Wanted To Know About Indians But Were Afraid To Ask.* St. Paul, MN: Borealis Books, 2012.

On the Internet

Discover Navajo
http://www.discovernavajo.com/

Go Native America
http://www.gonativeamerica.com/

Native American Music Awards: Rap/Hip-Hop
http://nativeamericanmusicawards.com/raphiphop.cfm

Navajo reservation

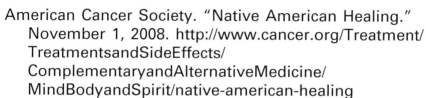

American Cancer Society. "Native American Healing." November 1, 2008. http://www.cancer.org/Treatment/ TreatmentsandSideEffects/ ComplementaryandAlternativeMedicine/ MindBodyandSpirit/native-american-healing

Boykin, Deborah. "Choctaw Indians in the 21st Century." *Mississippi History Now,* December 2002. http:// mshistorynow.mdah.state.ms.us/articles/10/ choctaw-indians-in-the-21st-century

Finger, John R. *Cherokee Americans.* Lincoln, NE: University of Nebraska Press, 1991.

Fonseca, Felicia, and Heather Clark. "Native American Doctors Blend Modern Care, Medicine Men." *USA Today,* September 16, 2010.

Fryman, Jessica. "Cultural Gap Inspires Mentor Group." *Las Vegas Review-Journal*, June 15, 2011.

Guillory, Raphael M., and Mimi Wolverton. "It's About Family: Native American Student Persistence in Higher Education." *The Journal for Higher Education,* vol. 79, January/February 2008.

Iverson, Peter. *The Navajo.* New York: Chelsea House, 2006.

Kraker, Daniel. "On Rural Navajo Reservation, Jobs Are Still Scarce." National Public Radio, October 21, 2009. http:// www.npr.org/templates/story/story.php?storyId=113967186

Morales, Laurel. "Coal Remains King on Navajo Nation—For Now." Fronteras, October 10, 2011. http://www. fronterasdesk.org/news/2011/oct/10/ clean-green-energy-pollution-electricity-plant/

Native American Aid: "Living Conditions." http://www. nrcprograms. org/site/PageServer?pagename=naa_livingconditions

Navajo Nation Department of Agriculture. http://www. agriculture.navajo-nsn.gov/

Nott, Robert. "Navajo Students Discuss Transition to College Outside the Reservation." *The Santa Fe New Mexican,* March 16, 2012.

Page, David. "Cherokee Nation Has 13 Oklahoma Students in Masters Degree Program." *Journal Record,* January 16, 2006.

PBS: "Historic Trauma May Be Causing Today's Health Crisis." *Indian Country Diaries,* September 2006. http://www.pbs.org/indiancountry/challenges/trauma.html

PBS: "Indian Removal." *Africans in America.* http://www.pbs.org/wgbh/aia/part4/4p2959.html

PBS: "The Trail of Tears." *Africans in America.* http://www.pbs.org/wgbh/aia/part4/4h1567.html

Potts, Leanne. "Hip-Hop Finds Audience on Reservations." *Chicago Tribune,* December 5, 2004.

Smith, Jessi. "Youth Explores Cherokee Life." *Herald-Tribune,* September 11, 2012.

Targeted News Service, "American Indian Spiritual Beliefs Influential in Spurring Youth to Avoid Drugs and Alcohol." August 20, 2012.

Trail of Tears: A Native American Documentary Collection. DVD. Golden Valley, MN: Mill Creek Entertainment, 2010.

United States Census Bureau. "American Indian and Alaska Native Heritage Month: November 2011." *Profile America Facts for Features,* November 1, 2011. http://www.census.gov/newsroom/releases/archives/facts_for_features_special_editions/cb11-ff22.html

US Department of Health and Human Services. "Alcoholism and Drug Abuse." *Minority Women's Health,* May 18, 2010. http://www.womenshealth.gov/minority-health/american-indians/alcoholism-drug-abuse.cfm

Wade, Jarrel. "Former Cherokee Principal Chief Chad Smith Looks Back With Pride." *Tulsa World,* October 25, 2011.

Wilmsen, Emily Narvaes. "Parental Behavior Regarding Alcohol is a Heavy Influence on American Indian Teenagers, Study Says." Colorado State University, June 28, 2011. http://www.news.colostate.edu/Release/5780

Wilson, Amber. "Cherokee Culture Promoted at National Tribal Holiday." *Tulsa World,* September 5, 2004.

casino (kuh-SEE-noh): a building used for entertainment, especially gambling

economy (ih-KON-uh-mee): the wealth, resources, and production of a region

grant (GRANT): a sum of money given to a person or group for a specific purpose

infrastructure (IN-fruh-struhk-cher): the basic systems that serve an area, including schools, transportation, and utilities

medicine man (MED-uh-sin MAN): a Native American believed to possess healing powers

migration (mahy-GREY-shuhn): the movement of a large number of people or animals to a new location

minority (my-NOR-ih-tee): the smaller in number of two or more groups

powwow (POU-wou): a Native American ceremony involving food, music, and dancing

ratify (RAT-uh-fayh): to confirm by expressing formal approval

reservation (rez-er-VEY-shuhn): a piece of land set apart for use by a particular group, such as an Indian tribe

sovereign (SOHV-rihn): having supreme power and authority

stereotype (STER-ee-uh-tahyp): a simplified impression of an entire group of people or things based on inaccurate or a small amount of information

treaty (TREE-tee): a formal agreement between two nations for the purpose of achieving peace